"Manuel is brilliant, and so handsome, too!"
—Manuel's Mom

"A beautiful book. Full of   all
need. You have learned th   lerful
teacher."
   —Bernie Siegel, MD, Author, *Love, Medicine & Miracles*

"This book will touch your heart, give you hope and strength
and the desire to share it with others"
—Mark Victor Hansen, Co-creator,
#1 *New York Times* best-selling series,
Chicken Soup for the Soul°

"This is a wonderful book about an important subject,
Inspiring and Helpful."
—Nido Qubein, CEO, Creative Services Inc.

"Your book, *Happiness Is a Pair of Shorts!*, is an inspirational
work of encouragement that would be excellent for anyone
facing challenges in their life, physical, mental or emotional."
—Ed Foreman, Former U.S. Congressman

"Inspirational, highly motivating, and sincere are just some
of the words to describe this book. Whether you, a family
member or loved one has been stricken with cancer, I'm
sure everyone can relate and draw strength from Manny's
experiences."
—Marcel Johnson, Brother in Christ & Friend for Life

"Your book was very inspiring to me and my class and my
teacher. When our teacher finished reading the book, we
asked her to read it to us again! P.S. Please come to St.
Matthews to talk."
—Daniel, Age 12

"Your story was so touching. You gave me such hope, inspiration, and courage. Thank you! Your story helped me get through the chemo treatments."
—Victoria, age 16

"Happiness Is a Pair of Shorts! is a wonderful saga, told by a unique and dynamic personality, Manuel Diotte. It is a personal story of pain and suffering and growth and development. In *Happiness Is a Pair of Shorts!*, you get a blend of "life offers us challenges" and "life offers us opportunities." Manuel encourages the reader to embrace the challenges and to search for the opportunities. It is a story that requires thought and reflection. It is a message that provides light projections and even deeper meanings.

As you read this special story, take on Manuel's manner and his greater challenges. That is:
* Reach for the stars * Experience it all
* Accept the joys * Learn from the defeats * Capture the moment * Chart a path * Focus your life * Perfect your goals * Enjoy your dreams * Live your life * AND
* Count it all a blessing!"
—Dr. Gloria "Jo" Floyd

HAPPINESS
IS A PAIR OF SHORTS!

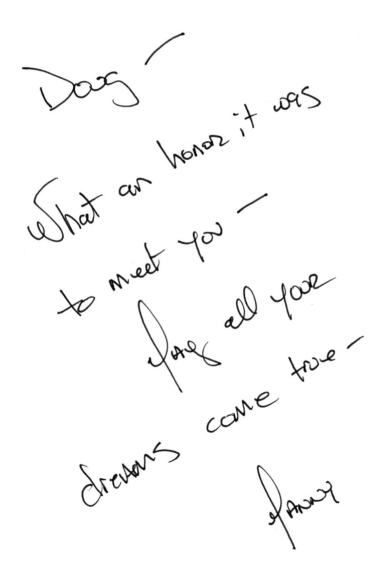

Doug —

What an honor it was
to meet you —

May all your
dreams come true —

Nanny

To contact the author with comments, or to inquire about speaking,
seminars, or consulting, write to:
manny@manueldiotte.com
info @manueldiotte.com

Published by
DARE TO DREAM

For additional products visit:
www.manueldiotte.com

Cover and book design: Jonathan Gullery

Library of Congress Control Number: 2001129225
ISBN: 0-9713692-0-8

Printed in the United States

MANUEL A. DIOTTE

HAPPINESS IS A PAIR OF SHORTS!

*Dealing with adversity through
Love, Hope, Faith and Courage.
Live your dreams...come what may!*

MANUEL A. DIOTTE

TABLE OF CONTENTS

Thalia Alicia Morin
April 4, 1996—August 2, 2000

HERE I AM…

WALKING A STRAIGHT AND NARROW PATH

TRYING MY BEST NOT TO TAKE A LEFT, BUT

WHAT IS THIS I SEE?

SOMETHING THICK FALLING OVER ME.

I CANNOT SEE WHAT IS AHEAD. I AM BLIND.

I DO NOT KNOW WHICH WAY TO GO…

DO I GO BACK? DO I GO FORWARD?

FEAR BEGINS TO SET, I CLOSE MY EYES AND I

CALL ON DADDY "PLEASE HELP ME?"

WHAT IS THIS I FEEL?

PEACE HAS COME OVER ME.

I OPEN MY EYES AND SEE A WARM BRIGHT LIGHT.

I HEAR A VOICE, SO SOFT AND GENTLE, FILLED…

FILLED WITH LOVE AND CARE.

"TAKE MY HAND AND DON'T LET GO, DON'T STOP

TO LOOK BACK. FOR I WILL GUIDE YOU SAFELY,

YOU SEE, THIS CLOUD WILL SOON BE BEHIND THEE

NEVER WILL I FORSAKE THEE, FOR I WILL ALWAYS

LOVE THEE"

WRITTEN BY VERONICA CANTU MORIN AS SHARED

BY HER DAUGHTER, THALIA ALICIA MORIN

Dedication

Eternal thanks
to the Prince of Peace, my Lord
and King, To my Savior who has gifted
and blessed me with the love and wisdom to
write this book.
To my Master who provides the peace that
passeth all understanding.
My friend, Jesus Christ.

To my mom and dad
who have been there during the most
challenging times in my life and who have shared
many tears with me. I love you to no end.

To my sister, Maria, and my brother, Daniel,
I love you and will never forget your support
during my countless tribulations.

To the doctors, nurses, staff, and custodians
who have cleaned my sheets, and wiped my body clean.
Thank you, I will never forget you.

To Dr. Melvin Smith & Dr. Koch, thank you
for keeping the faith and never giving up on me.

To all those involved in making this book a reality.
Thank you for your time, energy, hard work,
commitment, and dedication.

To the readers, may this book be
a source of encouragement for you
and a beacon of light on all that you hope for,
pray for, and believe to come true.
God bless you!

About the Book . . .

Hi, I'm Manuel Diotte. Before we get started, I'd like to share with you a story of what this book is all about.

There was a little boy who wanted to ride his bike with his friends. When he opened the garage door to get his bike out, he noticed that one of the tires was flat. So, he borrowed his dad's wrench and tried to loosen the nut in order to free the tire and patch the flat.

Despite his countless efforts, he just couldn't loosen the nut.

Then just before the little guy gave up, his father came walking out of the house and asked him what he was doing. The boy said, "I'm trying to loosen the nut so that I can take my tire off and fix my flat, but the nut holding down the tire is on too strong."

His father replied, "Are you using all your strength, son?"

The little one said, "Yes, sir." With a smile on his face, his daddy politely replied, "No, son you're not. You haven't asked me to help you yet."

I believe there's a lot we can learn from that story. You see, as a team, (that's **T-E-A-M**, which stands for Together Everyone Achieves More), we can be more productive. We never have to be alone. Together we will fill in the blanks. With your permission, I want to be that dad to help you, that coach to lift you up, that cheerleader to root for you, and that fan to stand by your side. Most importantly, I want to be your mentor and a friend that you can call on when you need words of encouragement. May God bless you, guide you, and always keep you in His care during your journey that starts when you ..... Dare to Dream!

—Manuel Diotte

Foreword

Manuel Diotte is a young man who not only has fought (and thus far won) the battle with cancer, he has also experienced challenges and disappointments that would have stopped many people in their tracks. He has been deceived and set back in business ventures in which he believed strongly and to which he gave his all. Yet, for whatever reasons, his hard work and expectations simply did not pay off. At this point, many people would have thrown up their hands in despair, saying, "What's the use? The deck is stacked against me." Surely Manuel must have felt that way himself on occasion. And yet he knew that inside of him were the seeds of faith that would nourish him to a happy conclusion and a story that would benefit and enrich the lives of others.

Manuel Diotte, though, is more than a survivor. He's a thriver, and though still a very young man, in many ways he has lived the life of a much older one as far as disappointments, betrayals, rejections and setbacks are concerned. *Happiness Is a Pair of Shorts!* is a book about overcoming. And through the grace of God, his undying faith, and his willingness to go not only the extra mile but to do whatever it takes to thrive and encourage, inspire and instruct others along the way, Manuel continues to overcome.

This is a book to be read slowly, carefully, digested, believed and followed. I encourage you to read it seriously, pray about it fervently, ask for the blessings that are contained within its pages, and believe you will receive those blessings, because God is faithful. He always hears prayer. Sometimes, of course, He answers immediately, sometimes His answer is "not now." Frequently He says no because "It's not in your best interests." Good news: When you don't understand God's head, you can always trust His heart. That message alone will bring joy and comfort to your life. Even as you may shed a few tears with Manuel along the way, they will be tears of joy and gratitude that say, "Yes, Lord, I know you are in

control and I'm grateful for that, because I know you will always act in the long-range best interests of your children."

When you finish this book you will pause for a moment and say, "If Manuel Diotte can overcome, so can I."

—Zig Ziglar,
Author and Motivational Teacher

CANCER IS BEATABLE, TREATABLE,
CURABLE AND SURVIVABLE.

Preface

Life! What a precious gift from God. In life, we are surrounded by many different sounds. However, there's no sound as beautiful as the sound of people laughing and enjoying life to its fullest, or of children giggling, living in their little world of fun, love, innocence and make believe.

Children are said to be the world's future. Yet many of them grow up too quickly when their innocence has been taken away and replaced with responsibility. Adversity strikes and this "gift" feels more like a curse. What happens to that child and that child's parents whose nightmare has become a reality? When their child, their healthy child, is ill? What happens to teens and adults whose world is now threatened many times with a challenge that requires everything from within them to survive? Many of them have thrown in the towel and given up on all their goals, dreams, and ambitions. They feel life is over and don't really know how to continue or why they should. They don't quite know how to turn a stumbling block into a stepping stone. Is there no help for them? The answer is yes, there is help. Yet many of them feel deprived and depressed and don't know where to look or turn for their answers. Many in our society would rather hear the negative, remember how life has done them wrong, and count the deaths rather than celebrate the births, count the victories, and take every experience as a blessing. There is good in everything, or at least, that's the way I see it. It may not be so obvious at first, but hang in there and believe me good will come.

"Why? Why? Why me?" we ask. Yet we never get an answer. Or do we? Are we not listening? What about the children, teenagers, and adults who struggle, fight and win? How about the countless number of people who use all their might and all their heart in beating the odds they had against them? Have we forgotten them? Sadly, many of us have.

Unfortunately, because of circumstances beyond our control,

THE GREATNESS OF OUR FEARS SHOWS US
THE LITTLENESS OF OUR FAITH.

we still lose many children and adults every year. We pray that the good Lord will take care of them.

Fortunately, because of advanced technology, much more knowledge is being gathered and many wonderful discoveries are being made every year resulting in thousands of people surviving. They're survivors!!! Winners!!! Call it luck, hope, faith or courage; they all have paid the price to live. The price is hurt, pain, and much suffering. However, there's a much greater price that some pay, the belief that they cannot continue to live a "normal" life.

I realize now, more than ever, that the real tragedy is not the illness or the challenge; it's the waste of that precious gift of life. So, now I realize I'm not **dying** of cancer; I'm **living** with cancer. It has made all the sense in the world, so this book is for all you winners who believe that you can overcome your challenges and live your dreams, because you can!!!!!

IF YOU DON'T THINK EVERYDAY'S A GOOD
DAY, JUST TRY MISSING ONE.

Introduction

A couple of years ago, I was registering my car, and as I was standing in line, a lady tapped me on the shoulder and said, "Excuse me. I don't mean to bother you, but aren't you the young man that was speaking downtown last week about coping with cancer?" I said, "Yes ma'am, I am." She then said, "I heard your good words and shared them with my daughter, who is very ill. I told her things will be okay, and I explained to her some of the great things you said, and I've never seen her happier. You've given her hope and reasons to fight. I can never thank you enough." I said, "Ma'am, you just did." I told her that hearing about her daughter's smile was all I needed. It's all the thanks in the world. I said, "It's like reading a book to a group of blind children. You can see their little smiles; you can hear their charming laughter, and inside you know that no amount of money can replace that feeling. It is I who should thank you."

I gave her my business card and told her I would be happy to speak with her daughter whenever she needed it. She never called and I never found out how her daughter was doing. However, it was then that I knew where the good Lord wanted me to focus my strength.

So a couple of years ago, I decided to write a book. I wanted to share my experience with the world so that others can learn and benefit from it.

I wanted to show others that we really don't **pay a price to live; instead, we enjoy the benefits of life.** Just as one doesn't pay the price of success, one enjoys the benefits of success. I wanted to show people that I was a winner, and that just having an illness or a challenge doesn't mean that you're going to die or that you have to stop living your life.

I am a winner, not just because I beat the odds, but a winner, because I hung in there, through thick and thin. A winner because I believed I could lead a normal life. As I started getting closer to

WE ALL HAVE DIFFERENT TALENTS, SKILLS, AND BLESSINGS. UNCOVER YOUR BLESSINGS AND MAXIMIZE YOUR POTENTIAL.

completing my book, I started to have second thoughts, the jitters, or something like that. I didn't want to share my life thus far with anyone. I started to become stingy. I felt it was too personal, and it brought back memories that weren't always pleasant. Some of it was even embarrassing.

Then, I thought of all the children. I thought of helping them. It became clear that it would be worth all the exposure in the world if I could just get one to smile, hear one laugh, or show one person a way to live a little better and a little more easily.

So, I started to write a book again. I decided not to make the book long for several reasons. First, I don't want to bore you with repetition. Second, I don't want to make this book a book about problems. Though I talk about some of my challenges, I want the real message to come out: That you *can* succeed, that we are all winners. Besides, the good Lord doesn't ever give us anything we can't handle. I don't want you to think about how life has done you wrong. We have to accept it and go on. It's the game of life with a different set of rules. Third, I want you to finish this book within a couple of nights because this book is designed to be a guide, to help you cope with your illness and challenges now, not next year.

This book was intentionally designed with enough space to write in the margins. Get a pen, pencil, or better yet, a highlighter or marker and get ready to mark, circle, underline, and highlight. Don't forget to write in the margins. Doing that will give you a quick reference later, instead of having to read the whole book again. If you need help or need to look something up, you can just go to the marked pages and refresh your memory on the materials that relate to you. Remember, this is *your* book and no one else's. It may sound selfish, but you may not want to lend this book out. Many of the notes you will write in the columns are obviously personal and you may or may not wish to share your thoughts or feelings with anyone else. So, only lend it out if you feel strong enough to let others read your personal comments. If you don't want them to read your remarks, just politely say, "I have personal points written in the book, so I'm sorry, but you

THESE ARE TRANQUILIZERS.
TAKE TWO BEFORE READING MY BILL!!

can't borrow it." They will understand and respect you for your wishes.

I hope you enjoy this book as much as I've enjoyed putting it together for you.

So please allow me to guide you through my life thus far. Let me share with you my trials and triumphs, in hopes of showing you a brighter path to your goals, dreams, and ambitions.

Well, get your **highlighter** ready and let's get started.

BE NOT AFRAID OF GOING SLOWLY;
BE ONLY AFRAID OF STANDING STILL.
—CHINESE PROVERB

Chapter One

Never Happen Captain
(Through the Eyes of a Six Year Old)

Not to me, no way. Cancer? Come on. I'm only six years old. I'm in the first grade. I just want to go to school, color, trade sandwiches at lunch, and play on the playground. Then, all I want to do is go home, ride my bike, catch bugs to show my mom, and play with my G.I. Joes until bedtime. I don't want any responsibilities; that's for grown ups.

I don't want to go to the hospital and have fifty million doctors look at me. They talk in a funny language that I don't understand. The last thing I need is to have them stick me with needles, take x-rays of my body, and hook me up to different machines that really don't make any sense to me.

I don't need that. I'm just a little person, a kid. I don't steal, lie, or hurt people. I haven't done anything bad except perhaps that time I scared my mom with a plastic snake. Boy was that funny, but I didn't mean to hurt her. Please don't hurt me. Come on. Pick on someone else—why me?

It's not fair. Why is it that little people have to go through such a hard time? It's bad enough I have to clean my room and keep my ant farm outside. I thought only bad guys had those hard problems. I promise to be nice to my sister from now on, really. All I want is to be better and not be sick all the time. I just don't understand—I better ask my mommy: Why? Why me?

"Well", mommy said, "it's not that you're a little stinker. Good people have problems and illnesses too." Mommy also said, "It doesn't matter whether we are big people or little people. God works in funny ways sometimes. There's a reason for everything, and one day you'll know why you got cancer." Sometimes I can't

WE GROW FROM ADVERSITY.

help but think of what my mommy said: "There's a reason for everything." I wonder what mine could be. Let's see. Maybe it's so I can have all the attention in school and I can be the most popular kid, with this cancer stuff. Yeah, that's it. So I can be the most popular kid in the whole school and in my neighborhood, too. That way everyone will love me. Oh no, wait a minute, what if it's so other kids can pick on me? I forgot I'll be bald with that chemotherapy stuff the doctor talked about. **COWABONGA CHEMOTHERAPY-YUCK!!!!! BALD!!!!!** What will I tell my friends? Oh, no! Maybe I won't have friends. Then what will I do? Mom!! Mommy!!! I don't want this cancer stuff. Can I give it away for FREE? Maybe I can share it with somebody, so they can be bald, too, and I can have a friend. Mom!! I don't want to be bald like daddy.

There has to be another reason. I can't wait 'till my daddy comes home, so I can ask him what he thinks my reason is. My daddy used to say something like...what did he say?...I don't remember exactly. He always said "Everything goes in one ear and out the other." I think he said my reason is so I can help other people one day. Yeah, that's it, so I can help other people. I knew that. Boy, I'll bet that's going to be great. Maybe I can be a spark in someone's life.

Imagine that. Having cancer isn't so bad after all. Maybe things can be okay for me and for everybody. I know, I'll write a book and tell everybody about myself, that "I'M A WINNER," and that things will be just fine. I'll even put a planner in this book. I mean, I just turned seven and the Doctor said I only had six months to live. I have to show everybody how to finish school in six months. I bet I'll be the smallest kid in high school. I bet there's lots of pretty girls—girls, did I say girls?—Yuck-o-la. I mean lots of sports. Sports is the only thing on my mind. I want to be a quarterback or someone important like the President of the United States. That would be so cool. Totally awesome! I can see it now:

ANYONE WHO THINKS MONEY IS EVERYTHING
HAS NEVER BEEN SICK.

MANUEL FOR PRESIDENT!!

I hope my mom and dad vote for me. If they don't that would be a real bummer. What about my goals, my dreams, and ambitions dad talked to me about? Ambitions. What were they again? Oh, yeah. How will I accomplish them? I'd better make this planner good. Well, I'd better go. I have lots to do. Dad, mom, I need your help with my ambitions.

As a kid your imagination can run wild. You can go from talking about cancer to wanting to be the next President without even knowing or understanding how short six months can be. That's innocence. Yet, we can all learn a lesson from a kid. We don't give up or stop living because of difficult circumstances. In the game of life, we will have many challenges. Mr. Murphy (i.e. Murphy's Law) will pay many visits. At times, his visit will hurt and call for everything we have in us to overcome the circumstances. Many times, when adversity hits, it can make us stronger and perhaps be the vehicle we need to take us to a higher level of growth. You see, if Mr. Murphy isn't visiting you today, he passed your door to visit someone else. We need to be prepared and have the right attitude to conquer the situations that arise. So when he decides to pay a visit, let's be ready. If you don't know who Mr. Murphy is, don't worry. He'll introduce himself. We won't have to ask, "Why me?" for we already know the answer. The answer is that the school of life is open to everyone, and that unless we learn how to overcome life's obstacles with the right mental attitude, many of us will never be part of the graduating class.

My friend the late, Mr. Dick Semaan would put it like this, "Don't let a negative attitude turn the stepping stones life sends your way into stumbling blocks." I agree with him 100%. When I was growing up with cancer I always looked at every situation in a positive way. Many of my parents' friends would say, "Manuel, you sure do have a great outlook on things, son." Or, "It's great that you're so optimistic about everything." Every once in a while I would hear those other comments like, "Positive nothing. God did you wrong, boy." Or, "What could you have possibly done to

BURY HIM IN THE SNOWS OF VALLEY FORGE
AND YOU HAVE GEORGE WASHINGTON.

deserve cancer?" Those statements were strong. Especially coming from adults. They hurt, and as a kid, I really didn't have an
answer. I just kept my faith. I prayed real hard every chance I
had and kept that positive attitude deep inside my soul, knowing
that the good Lord had a plan for me, and that whatever He was
doing, it would be for the good. I knew one day all my questions
would be answered. I never doubted God's love for me, and even
during the most awful circumstances I knew He was there for
me, and I was thankful for my very existence.

By the way, do me a favor. Put your hand over your heart. Go
ahead. Nobody's looking. Can you hear it? Listen. Listen closely.
It's your heart beating. It's God saying, "I love you" with every
beat. Listen. "I love you, I love you." God really does love you. It
amazes me, the number of people who'd rather point their fingers
at God or someone else, instead of acting responsible and search-
ing for solutions. I once heard that every time you point a finger
you have three fingers pointing back at you. So instead of blaming
someone or something, let's develop a winning attitude, move
forward, and stop trying to get even.

It doesn't matter what happens to us; it's what we decide to
do about it: point a finger or take responsibility. The choice is
ours, but in all fairness, I must tell you that nobody has ever erect-
ed a statue to a critic!

CALL HIM A SLOW LEARNER, RETARDED,
AND WRITE HIM OFF UNEDUCABLE,
AND YOU HAVE ALBERT EINSTEIN.

Chapter Two

A Year to Remember

It was Tuesday, May 20, 1969. Many great things happened that year. Man went to the moon. Richard Nixon was President (I know, I know). A three bedroom home cost about $25,600. A new Ford cost $3,278. Gas was $0.35 a gallon. Bread was $0.23 a loaf. In the World Series, it was the New York Mets over the Baltimore Orioles, and in Super Bowl III, New York beat Baltimore 16 to 7. In the world of medicine, the German measles (Rubella) vaccine was distributed worldwide. Most importantly, my favorite cartoon, 'Scooby Doo, Where Are You?' aired on television along with America's classic Sesame Street.

Best of all, a young man named Manuel Alfonso Diotte entered the world. I came in crying at about 10:15 in the morning, weighing in at eight pounds and seven ounces. I was twenty inches in length and as normal as could be. No challenges occurred before or during my mom's pregnancy. I was born in southern Spain, in a beautiful place called Granada. Spain is very special to me for I spent four years of my early childhood there. Shortly after my fourth birthday, we moved to the United States, where my father was stationed in Big Springs, Texas. Next thing I knew, it was 1976. I was six going on seven that year. I remember that year very well. It was the year I learned how to ride my bike without training wheels. It was also the year my sister and I built our first snowman together. It was the biggest on the block. Nineteen seventy six was also the year I was **blessed with cancer.**

My mother began to notice several bumps on my legs. At first we ignored them, because they would disappear. As active as I was, I had all kinds of cuts, bumps, and bruises. Then one day the bumps appeared again in the same spots. This time they were

HAVE HIM BORN OF PARENTS WHO SURVIVED A
NAZI CONCENTRATION CAMP, PARALYZE HIM
FROM THE WAIST DOWN WHEN HE IS FOUR AND
YOU HAVE A INCOMPARABLE CONCERT VIOLINIST,
ITZHAK PERLMAN.

painful. That's when my parents immediately rushed me to the United States Air Force hospital on Webb Air Force Base. The physician who did the physical examination noticed three swollen lymph nodes, the greatest dimension of the nodes being one centimeter. So, without hesitation, I underwent surgery. A brilliant surgeon, Bruce Bilder, a major in the Air Force, performed the operation. I underwent an excision biopsy. He removed a swollen lymph node for a biopsy. After the technician examined the node, they found nothing and couldn't explain the swelling. They sent me home. Over the next few months I started getting constant bloody noses. Many times, I was pulled out of school due to an unexplained high fever. Soon after, the swelling came back and spread to my left leg. The doctors immediately re-examined the previous surgical specimen (lymph node) held in the pathology department. The re-examination revealed what they called Lymphoid Hypersptasia. Then, after further review of the biopsy, they suspected that certain areas were suspicious with having Hodgkins Disease. On that same day, I underwent a right inguinal lymph node biopsy and bone marrow biopsy. In English, they removed fluids from my body to examine under a microscope. It turned out that the bone marrow (fluid) was negative. The lymph node tissue on the other hand, was positive, containing Nuclear Sclerosing Hodgkins Disease. On that day, the 17th of November, 1976, I was **blessed with cancer.**

Later that same month, I underwent a spleenectomy (removal of the spleen) and a staging (classification of how serious the cancer was). That operation resulted in my longest hospital stay: three months. However, I soon discovered that some folks stay in the hospital much, much longer. I had a tutor to help me daily during my long hospital stay so that I wouldn't fall behind in my school work. After the operation, they staged my cancer and I was placed in the category II A Hodgkins Disease. Hodgkins is classified in four stages. Each stage is broken into two categories. Stage IV B is the worst, and Stage I A is the least severe.

After the surgery, I was very ill. I was placed on penicillin, only to discover two days later, I was allergic to it. I broke out in

DEAFEN A GENIUS COMPOSER AND YOU HAVE
LUDWIG VAN BEETHOVEN.

a bad case of hives, and my entire body was covered in a rash. So, the doctors immediately placed me on Erythromycin as a substitute for penicillin. Two weeks after the spleenectomy, the doctors placed me on Cobalt Therapy (radiation treatment) in an inverted Y pattern with 3600 rads to the infected area. The inverted Y means they radiated down my legs. Later, they administered an accentuated dose of 4400 rads in the inguinal area (same area, just more radiation). I was to continue to receive radiation therapy with a total dosage to be given in a period of four to eight weeks. My father, who was in the military, was then transferred to San Antonio, Texas, on a humanitarian basis. I was then treated by Doctor Koch, who in my opinion was one of the finest pediatricians in the world. I was very fortunate to have such a good doctor on my side. After Cobalt was finished, Dr. Koch started me on Mopp chemotherapy. Respectfully, Dr. Koch is now retired.

My condition was not getting any better. It was then that Dr. Koch had a heart to heart talk with my parents and advised them that their little boy, who would be eight soon, had about six months to live. My parents, naturally, were heartbroken. They asked and begged that the doctors try anything, anything old, anything new, anything. They would have given their lives to save mine. As I struggled with my cancer, I continued to get smaller and smaller, losing a lot of weight. I was given more chemotherapy and more radiation treatment was ordered. In an effort to save my life, the doctors tried more surgery. The surgery was performed by talented surgeon, Dr. Melvin Smith. I believe that Dr. Smith was sincerely blessed and gifted with very special hands. Even so, time passed and nothing seemed to work. The chemotherapy was very strong and many times felt as bad as the disease. My parents, doctors, and friends prayed and prayed, in hopes of some sign of change. Nothing seemed to go right. Then it happened. The doctors ordered more tests, and after gathering in a room to look over the results, discovered that, just as everyone was about to give up, the cancer was getting smaller. This was a complete shock to everyone. The radiation started working and the cancer started to shrink. Everyone laughed and also cried.

RAISE IN ABJECT POVERTY AND
YOU HAVE
ABRAHAM LINCOLN.

Mr. And Mrs. Diotte's little boy had a chance. Praise God! Although the change was just the beginning of the fight, and many more difficult challenges were yet to come, this was truly a year we would all remember.

WE GET WHAT WE THINK ABOUT.
　　　—ORISON SWEYY MARDEN

Chapter Three

The Marathon

The difference between a marathon and a short race, like the 100-yard dash, is that in the 100-yard dash there's only one winner. In the marathon, *everyone* who finishes wins.

My marathon had started, whether I liked it or not, and it wasn't going to be just a 26 or 50 mile run. It turned out to be over two years of my childhood, and it challenges me even to this day.

I was sick a lot during those initial years and very weak. I was smaller than the other kids in my age group but my heart was bigger than my body. I just knew one day I would win and all the hurt would go away.

Part of winning the marathon was making sure I took my medicine as I was supposed to and I did. Even the glorious chemotherapy. Chemo and I didn't get along too well. I'd get sick to my stomach after the treatment. After all, the cure felt worse than the cancer. I remember when my dad would pick me up after school on Friday. We would go to the hospital for my weekly dose of chemotherapy. At that time McDonald's had hand puppets, and as a reward for finishing chemo, I would be given a puppet, so it made it fun. As you can already guess, yes, I collected them all, more than once.

Sometimes I would get candy, and I always would get love and support. Everyone around me was smiling and, not knowing any better, I would smile back.

My dad then took me home and let me watch T.V. The Incredible Hulk was always on, and I would watch Bill Bixby change into a big, green, strong monster. As I watched the Hulk, I would fall asleep, and the next thing I knew, it was Saturday morning, time for Scooby Doo, and I was once again feeling like a champ.

IT IS NOT THE MOUNTAIN WE CONQUER,
BUT OURSELVES.
— EDMUND HILLARY

Radiation treatment seemed to have worked very well with me. It didn't make me sick like the chemotherapy did. The kids teased me quite a bit that they wanted to use me as a tic-tac-toe board. After all, with all the red lines painted on me to mark the spots to treat with radiation, they just couldn't help themselves.

I called the radiation room "the tunnel of love." It was just me and this funny little machine that covered my body. I was always told not to move during treatment. Every time they would remind me, some part of my body like my nose, ears, or skin would start to itch. Nevertheless, somehow or other, I successfully completed all my radiation, and "the tunnel of love" and I have not seen each other since 1979. But I can't say I miss it.

To complete the marathon, surgery was in order. I have had over thirty operations. I think it's thirty four, but who's counting? I have to tell you, though, the most memorable operation was the one I call the M & M story.

I was scheduled for surgery and everyone knew that I would be in the hospital for approximately three months. The doctors prescribed O.T., better known as Occupational Therapy. This meant I got to make ceramics, belts, art, model cars, and whatever my little heart desired. It kept me busy during those long stays. I was eager to start a project, so I was sent straight down. Everyone in the room was working on leather and they were all making wrist bands. I thought I would do the same. I got my strip of leather and the letters in my name M-A-N-U-E-L. The therapist came by to help me and it was apparent that my wrist was too small for my complete name. I was hurt because I was told I wouldn't be able to make a wristband with my name. After all, I was little, and I didn't know any better. I got mad at the therapist, as though she had something to do with my wrist being so small.

Then, suddenly, someone yelled, "Manny! Put Manny on it. Besides that's the nickname for Manuel." My smile came back, but the therapist knew one less letter wouldn't really make a difference. So, she broke the news to me and I started to cry. Then the therapist shouted "M & M, Manuel, that's all you ever eat. You always have M & M's in your hands, your pockets, and your

THE MOST IMPORTANT PERSON TO BE
HONEST WITH IS YOURSELF.

mouth. That will be your nickname. What do you think?" M & M. Why not? I put it together and within minutes, I had my very own customized wristband. It's amazing what happens when we become creative.

Well the marathon wasn't over yet, but I must say I had a lot of help. So here's to all you M & M's out there—God loves you. Just hang in there and remember that it's the little things that we take for granted that we should really treasure the most. So, enjoy what you have and if you don't have it, don't charge it, because you probably don't need it anyway!

THE BEST TIME TO DO SOMETHING WORTHWHILE
IS BETWEEN YESTERDAY AND TOMORROW.

Chapter Four

Apply Within

I once read an old ancient proverb. It simply said,
"Master yourself and you can master anything."

WANTED:

Individuals wanted! Must have a good sense of humor and always smiling. Can be male or female, young, or old, should be fun-loving, caring, honest, determined, or goal-oriented. May be bald, ill, may have cancer, or be confined to a wheelchair. Must have hope, carry faith, and show courage. Must be strong, do what's right and have a big heart.

NEEDED IMMEDIATELY:

For lifetime commitment to great levels of excellence, to happiness, and to enrichment in daily life.

APPLY WITHIN:
ALL APPLICANTS ACCEPTED

Well, here it is, the formula that will not allow you to die, while you're living, because you have so much to offer. So many people die inside while they live. It's a tragedy that they have no self-appreciation. They give up just before things will get better—just before the tide turns, simply because they don't believe in themselves. People do not realize that they only lose when they quit.

I have a friend. If you were to meet him for the first time, you would later tell me that he's the most big-headed, conceited, egotistical snob, you've ever met in your life. All he does is brag about how good he is. All he talks about are his accomplishments.

COURAGE IS BEING THE ONLY ONE WHO KNOWS
YOU'RE AFRAID.

At times even I felt the same way, until one day when I took the time to talk to him and began to get a better understanding of his background. I soon discovered that his manner wasn't that he was big headed or conceited. It was that he believed in himself, even when others didn't. No matter what others said, he believed in himself. He risked everything he had to take a chance on his ideas, on his beliefs, on his goals, on his dreams and ambitions. He faced humiliation, embarrassment, laughter, and abandonment. Yet, despite all this, he went for it.

We all have so much to learn from this for we all need to have more appreciation of ourselves, our beliefs, and our abilities. We can start with our attitude, because as we face adversity, we will discover that our attitude is everything. Attitude will play a major role in determining how successful, or unsuccessful, we become. Whether it's obtaining a goal, winning the war on cancer, or mastering ourselves, a positive attitude will be one of our greatest assets **(remember this one)**.

Not only can attitude affect what we do, what we say, how we feel and look: attitude can also deeply affect how people around us act and feel. Our attitudes are contagious. Are you a carrier of a positive or negative one? Positive I hope! If not, strive to improve it. Surround yourself with positive people. Listen to motivational tapes and cassettes. Listen to people like Zig Ziglar, Les Brown, and, Nido Qubein and discover who they listened to and read about. As your awareness level rises, you can't help but become a more positive individual. The wonderful men and women in the speaking career field dedicate their lives to helping others learn and grow from what they have to offer.

Before I continue, I often refer to the word success or successful and I feel it is crucial that you know what I mean by success. So I'll share with you a passage I wrote while I was in college.

THE WORLD NEEDS MORE WARM HEARTS
AND FEWER HOT HEADS.

———⋙⋘———

SUCCESS

If you were to look up the word "success" in the dictionary, the dictionary would have defined it as attaining a goal, such as the attainment of wealth, the end of an endeavor that leads to reaching the top. Is that what "success" really is? I think not. I believe, rather, that success is a journey....not a destination. One doesn't wait for "success". He or she is successful every day during this journey. Each precious day that we are given is an experience and a challenge that enables us to grow and enrich our lives. A young lady fighting an illness, and winning, is successful during all her troublesome times, not just at the end. So is the man who builds a multimillion dollar company. He's successful from the beginning, whenever he is overcoming his stumbling blocks and trials along the way. So don't knock yourself down because you feel you haven't reached success yet, for as you continue your journey, you are already there.

Remember the power of positive thinking. In my office, I have a banner. It says, "I'M A WINNER". Being a winner isn't easy. I live up to that challenge daily. It requires a lot of patience, understanding, determination, and once again, that word: self-appreciation.

Not too long ago I was reading a book about Greek mythology and it talked about a courageous warrior named Achilles, the son of Peleus. According to the legend, Achilles was dipped into the river Styx by his mother in order to make him invincible and the bravest of all warriors. However, the water washed over all of his body except the heel from which his mother held him, leaving that one area vulnerable.

When Achilles' father was informed that his son would die in battle, he hid Achilles from the danger. The Greeks searched and searched for Achilles. When they found him, Achilles went to war to prove he was unstoppable, only later to discover that he was human. He died when his rival, Paris, shot a fatal arrow in his heel.

You see, Achilles' heel was his weakness. Yours may be the way you feel about yourself, your appearance, or your body. Don't allow your differences from others to control you. Get past what

HOPE IS FAITH HOLDING OUT ITS HANDS
IN THE DARK.

it is that holds you back. Get past your fears. Get past your fear of rejection because other people's negative opinions of you don't have to be your reality. You're better than that. You know it; I know it. Love yourself. It's okay. It's healthy and safe. Don't allow your Achilles Heel to be your downfall. Only when we dwell on our differences and *bring attention to them* will they cause a problem. This invites others to call attention to the differences as well.

A friend of mine has a scar on his left cheek. He is always picking at it, playing with it, trying so hard to cover it up. He's always talking about it and staring in the mirror. One day he was on a date with a girl he had liked for a long time. She knew he had a scar, but it had never bothered her. On the date, he drew so much attention to it, he ruined the entire evening. He kept saying, "Are you sure it's okay? I hope I'm not embarrassing you." She never cared about the scar. It didn't bother her at all. She enjoyed his company because she liked him as a person. She liked what was inside him. You could be the most beautiful person in the world, but if you're ugly inside, you're really not beautiful after all. The scar was obvious only to him, because he had no self-appreciation. He blew a great opportunity that could have been the start of a great relationship. Sometimes we do the same thing. We get so involved with our appearance that when opportunity knocks, we don't answer the door because we can't leave the bathroom mirror. My friend blew it because he can't care about and love another until he cares about and loves himself. The same is true about believing in yourself and others. How can you believe in others if you can't believe in yourself? Stop pretending! Stop fooling yourself! Stop lying to yourself! Take charge, because you truly are beautiful!!!!!!!!!!!

Remember that old saying? "Sticks and stones can break your bones but names can never hurt you." Well, they lied!!! Names do hurt. I know. But with a new feeling about yourself and your new outlook they can't hurt you because you know you're unique and wonderful! Don't become something that you're not and don't try to be someone else. When you put someone above you, you

FEAR IS A COWARD, IT ATTACKS
WHEN YOU ARE CONFUSED AND WEAK.

can only come in second even when you deserve to be first. Be yourself because you're special. Never stop believing yourself. You've heard of comparing an apple with an orange. That's what you do when you compare yourself with others. By comparing yourself to others you set yourself up for disappointment. Our differences build character and, most importantly, they make us original. I don't know the secret to success, but I know the secret to failure. The secret is, if you don't try you won't win!

The next time that you feel an insurmountable obstacle has beaten you, ask yourself "Did I stop because I failed or did I fail because I stopped?"

CHANGE IS THE ONLY THING
THAT OFFERS NEW OPPORTUNITY.
—ROSS SHAFER

Chapter Five

Time Out

In life, we have to overcome many obstacles. So many times, we give up just before we would have conquered, just before we were about to succeed.

For instance, one day I was speaking to a group of my friends about a baseball field. I told them that most baseball fields are covered with grass, except of course, the pitcher's mound, the baselines, and approximately 20 feet before the home run wall, which few people know about, referred to as the warning track. The 20 feet of dirt is there to warn the players that they're going to crash into the home run wall if they don't slow down. However, not all players pay attention to that warning and because of their willingness to succeed, some of baseball's greatest moments have occurred in that 20 feet.

Allow me to explain. An average player stops, freezes, pauses, or hesitates as soon as he sees the warning track and in doing so, allows an opportunity to go by because of his inability to adjust and expand his limits. On the other hand, the players who go out of the accepted boundaries and are willing to give it their all to go over and stretch beyond what is necessary to accomplish their goal of catching the ball instead of watching it go over the fence, these are the players that make baseball's greatest moments.

When an extraordinary player plays right field and a fly ball comes his way, I guarantee you they do not stop at the warning track. They run faster, jump higher, and they not only scale the wall, but also stretch their arms out as far as possible up and over the fence, and steal that home run. This is what makes them so exciting and great. That's why extraordinary players literally get paid millions to play. They won't be stopped by the limits others

IT'S NOT WHETHER YOU GET KNOCKED DOWN,
IT'S WHETHER YOU GET UP AGAIN.
    —VINCE LOMBARDI

set in their minds. They condition themselves to expand beyond the accepted area. They go out of the normal boundaries. We are only restricted by the limitations set in our minds. Our minds set limits on our abilities, our courage, our willingness to accept ourselves. If we are willing to take charge, take control, and not accept these limits, we will be able to achieve what it is we so strongly desire. Be creative, use your imagination, and turn your stumbling blocks into stepping stones.

Children are our greatest dreamers because they set no limitations on themselves. Many of us lose that creativity as we mature. We have so many limits set in our minds that we are unwilling to come out of our comfort zone. Eventually what happens is our "excuses" overwhelm our results. The reason children usually learn that they can't do something is that someone has come along and told them that it can't be done. "You can't do this; you can't do that." I'm sure you've heard it too. You remember the story about the choo-choo-train that said "I think I can, I think I can" as it was climbing a hill. Well, guess what? I know you can too. So go out there and better your best. Remember what Roger Gilbert Bannister accomplished in 1954. It had been determined by coaches and athletes all over the world that the mile could not be run in less than four minutes. The doctors had backed them up and had said that the human body could not endure a faster run.

Mr. Bannister, however, undoubtedly remembers the day when he did run the mile in less than four minutes. Mr. Bannister didn't accept the fact the mile had to be run in over four minutes.

He put all his heart into the effort and broke the world's record. He didn't moan and groan about how it could never be done. Mr. Bannister was determined. He broke a record that had been untouched for nine years.

This reminds me of the time I was bagging groceries. I was making good money, and a friend of mine wanted to work with me. So I told him that the boss hires every Tuesday, to be there early, and that I would put in a good word for him. Tuesday came around and the boss didn't have a job for him. He then waited

WE WON'T SURVIVE IF WE DON'T
FIRST BELIEVE WE WILL.

another week when the boss was going to hire another group. By the time the boss got to him, he had run out of name badges and said, "Sorry, son, maybe next time." So my buddy ran across the street, entered an engraving shop and bought a name badge. He had his name put on it and then ran back to see the boss. It had taken him less than thirty minutes to have it engraved and cost him less than three dollars, which paid for itself and then some, during his first hour of work, after, of course, the boss hired him. That's determination! We are all in this world together. No one being better than anyone else. Some of us are just a little more willing to go out and get what we want in life. We have to be determined. The goal or mark you want in life won't just be handed down. You must be willing to go out and fight for it. Fight and win. You must give it your all. You have to use all your heart, all your might, come what may! Many times we will face rejection, embarrassment, humiliation, and much criticism. So what! If you want the ultimate, you must be willing to accept what comes your way, to pay your dues, so that you can follow and cherish your dreams. In my case, I felt having cancer exempted me from everyone else's rules. But it doesn't. I am human too, and if I want to succeed and live my dreams, I have to fight for it myself. Only hard work and dedication will pan out. You have to have an unshakable amount of faith in yourself. Don't quit. Don't be tempted to take a short cut or the easy way out, because there is *no such way.*

Do you know what basketball, football, hockey, and all the great sports have in common? They all allow time outs. Even though the time outs are limited, they *are* allowed. In San Antonio, our NBA team is the San Antonio Spurs. I love to watch them play, especially The Admiral, David Robinson. When the Spurs are making one shot after another and the other team is losing its edge, the other team always calls a time out. The reason is to slow down the pace and to regroup. Notice, I didn't say the other team quits. They just need time to gather their thoughts and brainstorm. Sometimes that's what we have to do. We don't have to stop our lives, but instead, we just need to take a time-out

A DETERMINED PERSON IS ONE WHO, WHEN THEY GET TO THE END OF THEIR ROPE, TIES A KNOT AND HANGS ON.
—JOE L. GRIFFITH

and see where we are every now and then. Doing this allows us a chance to get organized. It allows us to see where we are and to focus on what we need to do to improve. Take the time-out opportunity to make necessary adjustments, not as a chance to slow down and give up.

Find your strengths. Improve your weaknesses. Stay focused and determined on what it is you're fighting for. Remember what you want to achieve. The beauty of it is that, in life, we aren't limited to the number of time-outs we can take. We can take as many as we need.

I BELIEVE THE ROAD TO PREEMINENT SUCCESS
IN ANY LINE IS TO MAKE YOURSELF
MASTER IN THAT LINE.
—ANDREW CARNEGIE

Chapter Six

The Twelve Minute Mile

It was my sophomore year in high school. It was the day we were all scheduled to take our physical examinations. I knew this day was coming and I was preparing for it. I sat down the night before and wrote out my goals for the day's events.

This was a day I would always remember **because for two solid years I had not worn shorts.** Due to the swelling and scars from surgery on my leg, I was scared of the teasing, so for two years I had kept that fear bottled up inside me. I had let that fear control me. Yet, that day it didn't matter anymore.

I was scheduled to run the mile and I was ready: shorts, heart and mind.

I no sooner got up to the starting line before I could hear the loud whispers, "Gross." "How fat." "How ugly!" I just blocked the whispers out and tried not to think about them. Then my coach yelled, "Ready, set, go!!!" I jetted out of there like an airplane, faster than anyone for the first twenty feet. I didn't know too much about pacing back then, but it was okay because I was determined to finish first.

As we came around the first of four laps, there were students all over the track. By the end of the second lap, many of the students had already quit. They gave up and were on the ground gasping for air. When the third lap came, I began limping and was on the track with only a few of my classmates.

By the time I hit the fourth lap, I was alone. Then it hit me. I realized that nobody had given up. Instead, everyone had already finished. As I ran that last lap I began to cry, as I realized that every boy and girl in my class had beaten me.

Everyone was staring at me and twelve minutes forty two seconds after starting, I crossed the finish line. I fell to the ground

USE THE PAST AS A SCHOOL,
NOT A BASEBALL BAT.

and shed what seemed to be oceans. I was so embarrassed. Suddenly, my coach ran up to me and picked me up, yelling, "You did it, Manuel. You did it, son!"Without thinking I replied, "I did what, coach?" He said, "Manuel, you finished, son. You finished!" He looked me straight in the eyes waving a piece of paper in his hand. It was my goal for the day, which I had handed him before class. I had forgotten. He read it aloud to everyone. It simply said, "I, Manuel Diotte, will finish the mile run tomorrow, come what may. No pain nor frustration can stop me for I am more than capable of finishing, and with God as my strength tomorrow I will finish." Signed Manuel Diotte, with a little smiling face inside the D as I always signed my name.

I said, "Thank you, coach." My heart lifted, my tears went away and I had a smile on my face as if I had eaten a banana sideways. My classmates all looked at me and applauded. They gave me my first standing ovation. It was then that I realized winning isn't always being first. Sometimes winning is just finishing.

There are several unknowns, mysteries, and challenges in life for all of us. How we deal with those times can be very difficult if we allow fear to stand in our path. So I ask you now, "What are you afraid of?"

Air:	Aerophobia
Work:	Ergasiophobia
Fish:	Ichthyophobia
Water:	Aquaphobia
Bees:	Apophobia
Frogs:	Batrachophobia
Ghosts:	Phasmophobia
Cats:	Ailurophobia
Cold:	Chromatophobia
Teeth:	Adontophobia
Spiders:	Arachnephobia
Snakes:	Ophidiophia
Time:	Chronophobia
Thunder:	Keraunnophobia

GREAT PEOPLE ARE JUST ORDINARY
PEOPLE WITH AN EXTRAORDINARY
AMOUNT OF DETERMINATION.

Light:	Photophobia
Colors:	Chromatophobia
Darkness:	Nyctophobnia
Dirt:	Mysophobia
Fire:	Pyrophobia
Rain:	Ombrophobia
Many things:	Polyphobia
Dolls:	Pediophobia
Change:	Neophobia
Robbers:	Harpazophobia
Germs:	Microphobia
Missiles:	Ballistrophobia
Trains:	Siderodromophobia
Sun:	Heliophobia
Wind:	Anemophobia

As you can see this list is a fraction of the many thousands of fears in life. Yet, as many as there may be, each and every one of these fears can be overcome, if we carefully examine them.

So where do *you* start? Good question, and I knew you would ask. You start with you. You start with believing in yourself and believing that you can get past your fears. You can do this by building a solid foundation. For many of us, this foundation will be spiritual. We will have the power of prayer, the power of our Maker beside us, and we will know we can overcome. We will know that we can handle any obstacle and face any fear. Some of us will build that foundation on the support of members of our family or special friends. These special people that we can trust and turn to are members of our encouragement club, members that will catch us when we fall, if we fall. Search and find those you want your encouragement club to consist of. Ask yourself: what kind of person am I becoming because of these friendships? The answer should be: a more powerful person who can grow in a positive way because of these relationships. Make your foundation reliable and strong with the right people as members.

CHANGE IS THE LAW OF LIFE.
—JOHN F. KENNEDY

It was St. Augustine who said, "Do what you can, and pray that God will give you the power to do what you cannot." In other words, you can do it all, if you're willing to put all your heart into it.

The point is we don't have to face fear alone. There are a lot of resources available to us, if we would just take the time to check them out. Remember T-E-A-M (Together Everyone Achieves More). When I was younger, I used to sleep with my back to the door. One night, I heard a sound and was so frightened that I feared turning around to see what it was. I then allowed my mind to play tricks on me and imagined the sound was a burglar and that he was in my room. I stayed still and wouldn't move for all the money in the world. I surely didn't turn around and face my fear. Instead, I soaked my bed with sweat.

My fear went on for three years. Sounds silly, right? Well, it was a nightmare for me. Finally, one day, I said: "I've had enough." I was sick and tired of being sick and tired. I felt like a coward. So, one night, when I imagined the burglar was there, I turned around and faced my fear, only to discover it was my parents, making sure I had covers on me before they went to bed. It had taken me three years to handle that fear. I remember having thought that if I was still and held my breath the burglar would think I was dead and leave me alone. It had been bad. After that I placed my bed in the room so that I had to face the door and my back was against the wall and I could see who was there. Even when I ate dinner in a restaurant I would sit at a table with my back against the wall so I could see out. I made a big mistake. I still allowed some fear to control me. I realized that fear is as big as we allow it to be, that it only has power when we give it power.

However, as I studied fear, I learned that not all fear is bad. Believe it or not, some fear is good. For example, if you're shopping and decide that you don't want to take advantage of a "five finger discount" because you might get caught. The fear of being caught is a good, legitimate fear. After all, criminal prosecution should not be taken lightly. It will guarantee to make you think

FEED YOUR FAITH AND YOUR DOUBTS
WILL STARVE TO DEATH.

twice before you carry out your mischief.

Another legitimate fear that comes to mind is the fear of report cards. If you know you'll be on restriction if your grades are failing or unsatisfactory, the fear of being on restriction can usually drive you to put a little extra effort into your performance.

Now, let's go back to examine some of the fears. Especially, those of us that haven't yet had the wonderful experience of chemotherapy, surgery, medicine, needles and so forth.

Remember when I said to examine our fears instead of complaining and wasting energy? We need to focus on some of the fears that limit us and start to grow. In order to accomplish our goals in life, we need to change or eliminate those fears. Once we learn not to accept limitations and become more energetic and creative in finding solutions, we can start eliminating our fears.

I remember when I feared chemotherapy because my doctor said there was a good chance that I would be bald. I'm sure you've heard it, too. I was only seven years old. Yet, I knew my friends would make fun of me. Even in high school when the students are supposed to be more mature, they teased me about my leg.

Later in life, I learned that the reason they made fun of me was that they had too much pride to ask what was wrong or what was causing my leg to be bigger or my hair to fall out. People often laugh and make fun of situations that they don't understand. Their ignorance causes them to hurt someone else because they don't understand and many times do not take the steps to find out why. My point is that you should not spend time worrying about other people's opinions. I've been hurt very badly. Don't listen to others trying to define or judge you. Your true friends will ask, try to understand and be supportive. Don't let irrational fear stand in your way. It took me two years to have the courage to wear shorts in public, two years I can never get back, two years I can reflect on and say: "I wish I could have worn shorts because I'm special, I'm somebody! You don't have to like me or my shorts and that's okay because I like me, and I have nothing to prove." You must be willing to come out of your shell. It will take some time, however, but you're worth it!! I know it,

IF YOU DON'T ENJOY WHAT YOU HAVE,
HOW COULD YOU BE HAPPIER WITH MORE?

and you know it. I believe in you and I know you believe in your-self or you would have never bought this book to guide you through troubled waters. Again I'm reminded of what Mr. Dick Semann once said: "A skilled sailor doesn't become skilled in a calm sea."

After an experience like overcoming cancer, everything else seems to be a cake walk on a beautiful Sunday afternoon. I faced the fear of death at seven years of age. No one thought I would live past another six months. I overcame that. If you can over-come the fear of death, what else is there? Nothing! Everything else can be handled. Most of our fears aren't life-threatening. If you can remember that, it surely will be easier to deal with the other fears. Is it going to be hard? Yes, it's often going to take all that you have to give, but aren't you worth it? Of course you are!!!!!

I'm reminded of another story of when I was bald and going to school. I discovered how awful little kids can be at times. Many times I was in tears when the kids at school called me names and teased me. The names referred to my bald head. Then one day four of my friends that lived in my neighborhood asked their moms if they could shave off their hair to be bald like me. They explained the best they could that they wanted to support me. Their mothers finally consented. So the school then had four plus mine, five, beautiful round shining bald heads. Some other kids became envious and asked their parents if they could shave their heads too. Suddenly, we had an epidemic at school of little bald heads everywhere. Not everyone's parents allowed it. However, a good number of parents did. I'll never forget that demonstration of support.

I recently heard of another event in which some high school students in Houston shaved their heads at a graduation in sup-port of one of the students. It brought tears to my eyes as I reflect-ed on my own memory. There sure are a lot of great people out there.

Later, the teachers at my school were instructed by the prin-cipal to talk to the students about me, and I was finally left alone.

YOUR ATTITUDE, NOT YOUR APTITUDE,
WILL DETERMINE YOUR ALTITUDE.
—ZIG ZIGLAR

But I remember what my friends had done. My suggestion to you is to take advantage of the situation! If you're a lady, and you're losing your hair, live it up, girl!!!! Turn that situation around. Did you know that wigs come in every color imaginable? Blonde, brunette, black, purple, orange, pink, and green, too. Find out if blondes really do have more fun. Did you also know that they come straight, curly, long, short, spiked, and so forth? Take advantage of it. Be a little crazy and wild! It's the 21st Century!! Purple hair is in!!! People will think that you're in! Then again, who cares what they think? Let them keep their negative opinions to themselves. It's your life. Take charge. Take control. Live it up! Remember what I said in the beginning. You've paid your dues to be here; that price being much pain and suffering. It's about time you enjoyed yourself. Of course, I'm joking. Don't go out and dye your hair purple unless you want to, but don't be afraid to live.

Most importantly, keep your self-confidence. Believe in yourself and in who you are, what you are, and what you stand for. A long time ago, I made a list of all my accomplishments. I invite you to do the same. By doing so you'll realize how many different fears you've faced before and remember how you overcame them. You can't forget those.

Remember, you did it in the past. Getting past fear wasn't easy then, either. Remember you have a foundation to stand on. It's okay to talk to and seek advice from your true friends, the members of your encouragement club. Many obstacles and fears can be overcome by solutions you yourself haven't thought of. It's true two heads are better than one, so use them to brainstorm and get ideas. Building a solid foundation takes time. There's an old saying: "A journey of a thousand miles begins with a single step." Results do not come immediately, either. Have patience. No one can be as hard on you as yourself. Be compassionate with yourself as you face your fears. Sometimes we make the wrong choices, and that's okay. It's called life. Learn from those experiences. At least when you try you're vastly better off than if you don't try at all. I'll say it again, I may not know the secret of success, but I do

WE LEARN AS MUCH FROM SORROW AS FROM JOY,
AS MUCH FROM ILLNESS AS FROM HEALTH, FROM
HANDICAP AS FROM ADVANTAGE- PERHAPS MORE.
——PETER BUCK

know the secret to failure. That is if you don't try, you can never win.

Be bold, be strong, and have the courage to take a chance on yourself. Courage is when you put fear aside and do what you want to do anyway. Courage is when you stand up to your fears and believe that you can do it. Courage is taking a stand for your self, come what may. Rejection, embarrassment, humiliation, so what? Courage allows us to take on fear face to face. Courage has allowed me to be me, not what everybody else wants me to be. It's not for sale. It's something we develop during our times of hardship, one step at a time, each step giving us confidence to take another step.

So many times, we play hide-and-seek from fear. Let me share with you a secret that I have discovered through my trials and tribulations. Fear will always find you, no matter where you are. So you might as well face it now.

Believe in yourself. Believe that you can. With the power of God behind you, you will overcome!!

STOPPING AT THIRD BASE ADDS NO MORE
TO THE SCORE THAN STRIKING OUT.

〰〰〰

Chapter Seven

Turning Lemons into Lemonade

During my teens, when I was a patient in the pediatrics ward, the nurses I grew up with asked me to put a magic show together. So I did. As I was performing in the playroom, a group of children, brothers and sisters, ran into the playroom. They were shouting, yelling at the top of their lungs, and crying things we couldn't understand, and just being very disruptive. I asked them to please calm down, and watch the show with the other children. As they continued to be disruptive, the other children in the room watching the show lost their concentration and I could tell the disturbance really bothered them. I couldn't take it any longer. My patience had run out and I finally yelled, "Stop it!" at the top of my lungs. Finally, their father, who had been down the hall, ran in the room and said, "I'm sorry. I wasn't paying attention. You see, they just lost their little baby sister, and I'm afraid they just don't know how to react." My heart, like yours, just hit the floor with sympathy and I just wanted to do anything to comfort him and the poor children. I wanted to do more than I could; more than I knew how.

I always reflected on that story when I felt that I had a problem, like the time I felt that being in the hospital for two weeks was forever. It was that day that I accepted my life despite the circumstances. I will never again take any day in my life for granted. Now, no matter how bad things may seem, I understand that in reality there are people worse off than I. Here I was, fighting a disease I couldn't even spell, and thinking it was the end of the world, and that man's daughter didn't even have a chance to live. I can't help but think of the silly things we argue or get upset about and blow out of proportion. For example, leaving clothes

COURAGE IS NOT THE ABSENCE OF FEAR,
BUT THE CONQUEST OF IT.

on the floor and forgetting to pick them up, or leaving the toilet seat up (that one drives my wife crazy). It really makes us think. Since the day of my magic show, I live by certain golden rules. Rule one, do not sweat the small stuff. Rule two, it's almost all small stuff.

So now that I've decided that I need to stop complaining about the things I can't do because of my cancer, I am able to focus on things that I can do. By the way, you don't have to have cancer to appreciate this advice. Life is a challenge in itself. Therefore, this advice applies to life, too. I can remember when I was selling real estate and some of the agents (usually the non-producers) were always complaining about how bad the market was. I would always hear them say things like, "Sure is a slow market." Or "People just don't want to buy or sell anymore." Or "We must be in a recession." Yet, every day houses were being marketed and sold by the top agents. Why? Mainly because the top agents adjusted to a change in the market. They changed the rules. They became more determined and more focused. The non-producers came in at 10:00 a.m., sat and talked about how bad the market was and how life had done them wrong. They talked over a pot or two or three of coffee. Next thing they knew it was time for lunch. For lunch they went out with other agents, as if another agent were going to buy a house from them. They got back about 3:00 p.m. or so, complained some more and decided to leave at 4:30 p.m. so they could miss the five o'clock traffic. Five o'clock traffic heck. They missed the boat! The next day they repeated this and the next day, and the next.

While they did that, the top producers were selling and marketing. They accepted the market and decided not to participate in the recession, so to speak. The way I saw it is that 50% of the agents quit during tough times. So that left twice as much business for those willing to work.

Cancer works in the same way. Don't set limitations for yourself. Do not, I repeat, do not dwell on what you can't do or change. You have to accept the market, the situation, yourself. Denying that it exists will only hurt you more. Feel what pain

COMMITMENT GIVES US NEW POWER. NO MATTER
WHAT COMES TO US— SICKNESS, POVERTY,
OR DISASTER, WE NEVER TURN OUR EYE
FROM THE GOAL.
            —ED MCELROY

you must, shed the oceans you must shed, and go on with your life. You might be saying, "Manuel, that's cold! You have some nerve putting it that way." Well, you're right, but cancer is colder. So, you can allow it to hold you, or you can let it go. From experience, it is better to let go. Don't let yourself die inside. You have so much to give, so much to look forward to. You have goals, dreams and ambitions. I know you do. In a later chapter, I'll show you how to obtain them. First, you have to learn to accept yourself, believe in yourself, and decide right now, that "Yes, I want to eliminate my fear and live my dreams!"

I want to share another story with you. My cancer was cured by an overdose in radiation. The overdose ended up burning my right leg, causing the vessels and canals in my leg that help circulate my bodily fluids to collapse. As a result of the overdose, my right leg is double the normal size, making it very difficult to walk at times. It is even harder to put on clothes, such as a pair of jeans. (In Texas, you *have* to have jeans!) However, after my sixteenth operation they reduced the size of my right leg and made it close to the size of my left leg. I remember that operation very well because I had always wanted to have a pair of boots. (In Texas, you *have* to have boots!) That summer (of 1988) I bought my first pair of boots. They were a size twelve triple E. Big right!? Well, to tell you the truth, they could have been a sixteen Quadruple E and I would have loved them just as much. I was overwhelmed to have a pair. It's funny what makes a person happy after an experience with cancer. I, like you, decided I had better turn the table and stop complaining. I mean today! Right now! There are people without feet who would love my big leg. Since my leg is big, I always have to wear my right shoe bigger than my left. You see, I got the opportunity to convince the salesman to sell me two sizes for the price of one, like mixing and matching an outfit. I get to pick a size ten for my left leg and a ten and half for my right. Does it work? I have been successful twice. What a deal!

I know what you're thinking. This guy can do everything right. Wrong! You see, a big leg has its disadvantages. I just prefer

DON'T BE AFRAID TO GO OUT ON A LIMB.
THAT'S WHERE THE FRUIT IS.

not to think about them. For example, when it comes to sports, I have a real hard time running. My leg gets so swollen it is difficult for me to run. I never complain about it because it's like I said before, so many people just wish they could walk! I'm thankful I can run at any speed, fast or slow. After all, it's a miracle I'm even here!

I have realized cancer isn't the end of the world and that there's more to life than dwelling on the negative. There is more to life than complaining that I can't be on the football team. After all, I still enjoy watching sports, and playing, too. I just have to know when to stop. I know when to say, "okay guys, my leg has had enough". All my friends respect me for that. They never get upset because I have to leave, even if the teams will be unequal.

Since I wanted to be active in something, I decided to get into sales. I consider myself an exceptional salesman. I take care of my customers, and they take care of me. In high school, I made top salesman four consecutive years. During the fund raisers, I sold more candy and novelties in two days than the other kids combined did in two weeks. Boy, was I proud, not to mention the fund-raising committee. Since a career in sports was out of the question, I decided to make a choice – the same choice many of you will make. You can show the world what you can do or hide and decide to waste your life and appear on talk shows telling people how life did you wrong. That's a real hard decision, huh? It is for many people. It's a good thing you're not one of them. When you picked up this book, you took the first step to teaching yourself that you can get past your fears and live your dreams. You took a chance on learning and on developing yourself.

Besides sales, I also started taking acting in school. I advanced to the senior class in drama by the end of my freshman year. In my spare time, to stay off my legs, I started collecting key chains, stamps, coins, stickers, comics, and sports cards. I just had to live it up. As if that were not enough, for a kid that was given a death sentence, I became the youngest REALTOR in the State of Texas in December of 1987, at the age of eighteen. I was in the papers as a teenage REALTOR. Boy, was I ever excited! I received

YOU MUST FIRST BE A BELIEVER IN
ORDER TO BE AN ACHIEVER.

phone calls from all over the state to try to recruit me and to congratulate me as well.

In 1989, I formed two companies and incorporated them both. I had a small mail order business which I ran on my own and a badge-making business which I managed and in which I had students working for me. I also have a patent in Washington, D.C. which was granted in November of 1990 by the U.S. patent office. In addition, I graduated from high school with honors and two scholarships. One scholarship was for writing and the other was for a personal interview. The interview was about my goals and attitude in life. I could have written all the bad things that had happened to me too, but I decided not to. I wanted to share with you some of my triumphs, more so than my tribulations. Even though at times it seems easier to remember the bad, I think the good sounds much better. Wouldn't you agree?

Today I am a professional speaker, author and entrepreneur and still maintain my real estate license. My goal is to act as a catalyst and make an incredible difference in the quality of people's lives. I want to leave people better than I found them and say something that will let them breathe easier, and eventually they can say, **"I am living my dreams"** as I live mine. Meanwhile, I'm thankful for being able to work and to be productive until I reach my dreams, my ambitions, my destiny. So, ask me if I mind having had cancer and a challenging leg. No! No way! It has been a challenge, a test, and I'm passing! It has helped me become the person that I am. If I never had that experience, I would not have written this book and I could not have shared with you what I have. No, I don't mind. I'm glad it was me, because I would never have wished cancer on anyone else. God has a plan for me. Even though I didn't understand it then, it's clear now.

You just have to believe it's all for a reason. If you don't know the reason, just give it time, and understanding will follow. The choice is ours. Some of us will believe, and some of us will not believe that it all happened for a reason. I guarantee you, it's easier to believe what happened and accept it, then to reject or deny or never understand.

THE ONLY THING WORSE THAN A QUITTER
IS THE PERSON WHO IS AFRAID TO START.

Another challenge I faced was that as I became closer to some of my friends, they began to ask me about my leg and medical condition. Discussing my medical history was difficult. Remember when I said people who made fun of my leg were ignorant for not asking? Well, now that they asked it made me feel uncomfortable. They asked to learn and they wanted to be educated about what they did not know, but I was scared. I was scared that they might not accept me anymore. Then one day a close friend of mine asked me, "why do you always say that you are blessed with cancer?" It was then that I started to feel comfortable talking about my situation and answered the question by saying that during my experience with cancer, many wonderful things have happened, many of which would never have occurred unless I was blessed. Saying I was blessed helped me believe that there is a purpose, a reason to fight and go on. I wasn't scared anymore. It felt good to talk about it with someone close to me. My friends, parents, and doctors all helped me win this battle. It also took a lot of faith on my part, which, as you will discover later as you read, is an important ingredient in my life.

You see, if we can believe in the fear of the unknown so strongly, why is it that we have such a hard time believing in the faith that's unseen? I've always been a believer. I've always believed that I could instead of that I could not. I believe it's my faith that has carried me through troubled waters, my faith in God, my faith in myself. So you've tried and failed. So try again. Walt Disney failed seven times before he was successful. Look at Thomas Edison. He learned 10,000 reasons why and how a light bulb didn't work. However, he also learned the one that made it work, *because he believed.* He would not quit. He had an unshakable amount of faith; he believed he could. Let's not forget about great sports figures, such as Babe Ruth. He led the league in number of strike outs, but he also led the league in number of home runs. These great people succeeded because they believed they could.

TEAMWORK BREEDS MORE
PRODUCTIVITY.

Fact: it takes more muscles to frown than to smile. It also takes less energy to work really hard and do something right than to make excuses when you get it wrong, because you didn't work at it properly.

Work hard, work smart, and stop comparing, criticizing, and complaining.

TO GROW TALL SPIRITUALLY, A MAN MUST
FIRST LEARN TO KNEEL.

Chapter Eight

It Only Hurts When I Laugh

My doctor once said, "Manuel, how do you feel?" I replied, "With my hands." He sent me home. When I was little, I believed that all stars were guardian angels and that a shooting star was a guardian angel going to work. I used to believe in this very strongly. As a matter of fact, I still do. It's silly perhaps, but with something as serious as cancer we all need something in which we can believe or someone to keep us going. Lucky for me I had both. I've always had my guardian angel watching over me during the day and the night. I could always see my angel, I knew he was there. As for the other part, the someone, I also had a lot of "someones" pulling for me. I started what I called the encouragement club. Since I'm the President, Owner, and Chief Executive Officer, I allowed myself the authority to give out exclusive memberships. Not everyone was allowed, especially not those negative thinking people we talked about earlier. You remember, the ones who have nothing better to do than complain. They waste their energy telling us their problems instead of masterminding solutions, and at the same time drain us of our energy. While other people are dealing with chemotherapy, radiation and surgery, they're complaining because their lipstick doesn't match their socks and underwear or because the movie they wanted to see was sold out. You would think they would learn to have a back up plan to go do something else instead of wasting time complaining. Well, enough on the non-members. Let's talk about my exclusive members, like my mom and dad.

Remember when I said you need to build a foundation first by believing in yourself and having faith. Now it's time to make that foundation stronger with the members of your fan club. I'll

LET US PRAY, NOT FOR LIGHTER BURDENS,
BUT FOR STRONGER BACKS.

start with my mom, Maria Lourdres. My mom was born in Spain, like me. She was raised there with eleven members of her family. She lived in a three bedroom house with her grandparents and nine brothers and sisters. Yes, nine, all sharing a small three bedroom house. You can compare it to a small modern day apartment. Not big at all, just enough room to eat and sleep and sometimes feel comfortable, when most of the family was out working. They were so poor that they couldn't afford a watchdog. When they heard a noise at night they would start barking. I'm kidding, of course, about the barking, but things weren't easy for them. However, no matter how bad they had it, they had each other. They were rich with love. They had food every day (and plenty), as well as a roof over their heads every night. The family was very close. At the end of the day, no questions were left unanswered. Every problem was solved, for unity was extremely important. They would help each other, all the time, every day. My aunts and uncles would go to work, and when they came home they would pool their money together to help my grandparents with the bills and house payment. Helping each other is still a family tradition. My mother was very lucky to be brought up in such a loving family.

My mom is a very strong person. She has survived the toughest of times with me. She stayed up night after night, with little to no sleep, worrying. She spent countless nights in the hospital, resting on an uncomfortable chair, making sure my stay was as pleasant as possible. I remember my mom saying over and over, "I wish I had your cancer, and you could be okay." I would always respond by saying, "No way, I got it. It's mine and I'll be just fine. Besides, I can handle it." I would never show fear or show any sign that I was ever scared while I was in the hospital. I just hated to worry my mother. No matter how bad I felt I would never show it. However, my mom knew me like the palm of her hand. Rarely did I sneak one past her. If I was not my optimistic self, she would instantly know and give me so much love it gives the word a whole new meaning. Mom, I love you.

Next, is my father Gerald Richard Diotte. My dad was born in

GOOD THINGS MIGHT COME TO THOSE WHO WAIT,
BUT ONLY THOSE THINGS LEFT OVER BY
THOSE WHO HUSTLE.
—ABRAHAM LINCOLN

White Plains, New York. He grew up on a farm and milked cows in the early hours of the morning before he had to walk to school, uphill, both ways in eight inches of snow. Many of you have heard the story before. Just kiddin', dad! My father has been an inspiration to me. He has always been a hard worker, and dedicated to his job. Like many fathers, he works all day.

My dad's special. He works all day not because he has to, but because he wants to give everything he can to our family. He wanted us to have the luxuries in life, like food and shelter (joke intended). He wanted us to be in good schools and in a better environment. My dad is gentle and compassionate. His heart is bigger than his life. My dad goes out of his way to help people. There are takers in life and there are givers. He's a true giver. I used to tell my friends if they were to look up the word *giver* in the dictionary, there would be a picture of my dad. Growing up with my dad was wonderful, he taught me bad from good. He passed on to me many great morals and values which will stay with me forever. One value that comes to mind is to respect everyone. He means the world to me and I could never let him down.

My father is very strong, yet emotional. But you'll never see him cry. I was eighteen years old going in for my sixteenth operation. It was the first year I was authorized to sign my own consent form for surgery. This is the form that tells you that you can die or develop complications or the surgery may result in any of the fifty thousand side effects listed below, such as, too much anesthesia, too little anesthesia, heart problems, brain problems, and so on. As I read this I cried. I cried not because of what could happen, but because my parents had to sign this form for their little boy fifteen times before. I looked at my dad and it was the first time I saw his eyes water. As I signed it I felt an incredible fear. The same fear that they had dealt with in the past as they signed the form – the fear of the unknown. My dad comforted me and he asked if I was sure, I said, "Yes, Dad" and his tears rolled down his cheeks, landing on the side of my face as he hugged me and said "I'm proud of you, son." I'll never forget the love and

WHAT MAN DOES FOR HIMSELF, HE TAKES WITH HIM. WHAT HE DOES FOR OTHERS, HE LEAVES BEHIND.

support my dad has given me. That can never be taken away. I love you, Dad.

Approximately 1 year, 6 months, 26 days, 2 hours, 45 minutes, and 17 seconds after I was born, my little sister, Maria, entered the world. Having a baby sister was probably the best thing in the world that could have happened to me even though I didn't realize it at the time. However, I later realized the love and support she gave to me. Everywhere my sister went, I went, and vice-versa. We were always together, holding hands and watching out for each other.

Maria was the kind of sister that could go watch paint dry and be excited because I was there with her. What's ironic is, I remember the times we both were in trouble and as much as we cared for each other neither one of us would take the blame. Regardless of who was at fault we would never admit our guilt. That held true during our teenage years as well.

During my experience with cancer Maria was always real close to me. I thank the Lord, because I probably wouldn't have made it without her. Maria would always protect me during my treatment.

I remember the first day, when I went to school bald. I was teased and teased. The kids would not stop till they made me cry. One of my classmates was teasing me and running around me, trying to hit my bald head. Maria came over and chased him off. It was funny that my little six-year-old sister was willing to stand up for me. She had more guts than a seven-year-old coward who had nothing better to do than to hurt me by calling me names. Maria protected me all the time, even when I was better. It's the little things she did that kept the spark inside of me alive. I love you, Maria.

Then there's my brother, Daniel, who could charm a bird down from a tree. One of the happiest days in my life was the day he was born.

Daniel has always looked up to me. I've been his role model. Being a role model brings out a great deal of responsibility in me. Daniel is super sweet, a real gentleman. Though Daniel wasn't

THE TRAGEDY OF LIFE IS NOT THAT IT ENDS
SO SOON, BUT THAT WE WAIT SO LONG
TO BEGIN IT.

born until after I was cured, he still is a very important part of my foundation. Daniel didn't understand cancer at his young age but he does understand being sick, especially since he had asthma. We were even hospitalized at the same time once. My mom was going from one floor to the other, keeping an eye on us. His asthma got much better as he started to outgrow it. Daniel is very caring. He would always make sure that, when his friends were all playing ball, everyone would play, even if the teams were uneven. He's got a lot of heart.

One day I was stuck at the hospital and I wasn't allowed out on pass. My family had made plans with friends, and they had thought for sure they could get me out on pass. They couldn't and I told them to go without me. Well, they went, except for Daniel. Daniel was only nine at the time. I told him to go but he insisted on staying. I told him he would be bored and he said, "No way, not with you here." So he stayed and he got a pillow and jumped up on the bed with me, and we both started to watch the football game that was on. It wasn't even halftime and Daniel was out cold. Bored to sleep. I couldn't stop laughing 'cause he had made such a big scene in order to stay. He slept almost four hours before my parents came and got him. I'll never forget that day. The fact that he slept didn't matter. The importance was that his intent, at nine years of age, was extraordinary. Daniel, I love you.

Remember to build your foundation with the understanding that we may not always know the answers, but if we hang in there as a team, it is amazing what we can accomplish.

Have fun and smile. Humor plays a big role in my life. It helps me deal with the pain, and it keeps me going, allowing me to look forward to the challenges that lie ahead. Try humor. After all, what do you have to lose?

Next time you run into a group of bald friends say "Guys, I heard a joke today that will knock your hair off." (Look at their heads and say) "Oh man, I guess you already heard it!!!!!"

THERE ARE TWO KINDS OF PEOPLE--—
THOSE WHO HAVE ULCERS AND THOSE
WHO GIVE THEM.

Chapter Nine

The Power of Faith

I was in the hospital and overheard a doctor talking with his patient. The patient explained that he was having a hard time trying to sleep. The doctor suggested that all he would have to do was hire a beautiful nurse and have her "kiss you every fifteen minutes." With a big smile on his face the patient said, "That's it, that will put me to sleep." The doctor replied, "No, sir, it won't, but it sure will be a pleasure to stay awake." Now, that doctor has the right attitude. Speaking of attitude, I'd like to start this chapter with a question. The question will shock some of you. Many of you will find it profound and most of you will say "Boy, oh, boy. Manuel's got some nerve. He must have a good day every day."

The question is simple. Here it is:

Is your attitude worth catching?

That's a strong question I'll agree, but I've seen time and time again, that study after study, interview after interview, and survey after survey of the leading professionals in the world revealed that a positive attitude was directly related to their position of success and/or happiness in their life.

You see, a positive attitude lets us see a glass half-full, not half-empty. It lets us see the challenge, not the problem. It lets us count our victories not our tribulations. A positive attitude has played a key role in many lives. Ann Jillian, Lee Iacocca, Honorable Clarence Thomas, Helen Keller, Dr. Martin Luther King, Walt Disney, Barbara Bush, Dr. Norman Vincent Peale, _____ (enter your name), and the list goes on.

Let me ask you again, is *your* attitude worth catching? I believe it is. It's your positive attitude that led you to buy this book. It's your positive attitude that will let you conquer your challenges. And it's your positive attitude that will let you become the success that you're destined to become.

THERE ARE MANY WAYS TO FAIL:
NOT TAKING A CHANCE
SEEMS TO BE THE MOST SUCCESSFUL.

In a nutshell, I quote the most positive man I've had the honor to meet, master motivator Mr. Zig Ziglar. He said, "A positive attitude won't get you anything…but it will get you everything better than a negative attitude will." Yes, my friends every day is a good day, and if you don't believe me just try missing one.

As I am writing this book, I'm 32 years old. It's incredible for me to realize that twenty-five years ago I was given six months to live. I feel that I am the luckiest man in the world. I guess anyone who has had over thirty operations, radiation treatment, eighteen months of intense chemotherapy, been stuck with needles over 2,800 times and has spent over three years of his young life in a hospital has the right to say he's lucky. The truth of the matter is that I am not really lucky. I really am blessed.

It's a tragedy to think that so many people don't appreciate what they have until it's gone. Don't ever let that happen to you. Appreciate every day. With the right attitude, see the opportunities that lie ahead. Thank God for the sun, the rain, the stars, the moon, the good, the bad, and the ugly, because, deep inside your soul, if you really care to look, you will find that there is good in it somewhere. And I really believe, deep in my heart of hearts, that if you have faith and a burning desire, whatever you must go through to make life better for you is worth it.

Speaking of faith, I was at the SUCCESS 1993 seminar in San Antonio and was speaking with Peter Lowe, one of the speakers. He said something that we can all benefit from. He said, "Fear knocked, Faith answered *and no one was at the door.*" My friends, that's powerful. That's faith in action. That's the kind of faith we need to develop. True faith makes fear vanish completely. We must have faith in our God and in our abilities. We must have the courage necessary to put fear aside and do what we so strongly desire! No matter what!

"BUZZ, BUZZ, BUZZ" GOES THE OPPORTUNITY CLOCK AT 5:30 IN THE MORNING, IN 1985. It would continue to do that for the next two years. The swelling in my legs caused me to limp very badly. Many times, I would have to sit in a wheelchair because of the pain. It hurt to walk. So for two years I went to

TROUBLE IS WHAT GIVES A FELLOW A
CHANCE TO DISCOVER HIS STRENGTH
OR LACK OF IT.

physical therapy and had my leg massaged (cool, huh?), so that my leg would not give out on me. I've fallen down so many times that I can't keep count anymore, and really don't want to. Bright and early, I was off to the hospital for therapy. I say early, because, for a high school kid, 5:30 a.m. is unheard of. You talk about the early bird; I was the early worm. However, I had to go early because school started right after therapy. I went faithfully every day except the weekends, because I had an unshakable faith that I would get better. I kept that faith alive and very much in me every day in my prayers. I just *knew* one day I would walk without a limp.

As you can see, faith is very important to me. Fact is, it is extremely important to me. It lets me believe that whatever I must go through will be worth it and that my reasons or purpose are worth the time, energy, and dedication.

So I say to you; be thankful for adversity for it brings the faith out in you.

Believe me, friend, faith is beautiful, even if unseen. Be glad that you're where you are and that you can be where you want to be, if you just believe that you can. My friend Charly said something that we can learn from. He said, "Life is like a merry-go-round, because it's comfortable, predictable. Everything is always constant and everything always stays the same. It does not require much effort or risk. The roller-coaster, on the other hand involves some risk. It has its ups and downs, but if you hang in there, you know you will make it to the top and the view from the top is magnificent. The irony is, no matter which one you choose they both will have highs and lows. So you might as well jump on the roller-coaster and fasten your seat-belt and have a good time."

Besides, you have the faith within you! You're unstoppable! You're unique! You're fantastic! You're incredible! You were born to win because God doesn't make junk! He just doesn't!

DON'T FORGET THAT APPRECIATION
IS ALWAYS APPRECIATED.

Chapter Ten

Dreams, Goals & Ambitions

Now that we know the power of a positive attitude and the importance of faith, let's discuss your future. This chapter is a lengthy one, so let's get started.

Whether big or small, long term or short term, we should all have goals. Goals give us a sense of direction. Goals along with a plan of action can lead to a great sense of achievement and fulfillment.

However, goals are like knowledge; useless, unless you apply what you know. Anything worth attaining is worth committing too.

Whatever your goals, it's important to realize that they are not set in stone. Your individual situation will change, so many of your goals will need to change as well. Many times, we change the direction we're going, but we forget to change our goals. It seems easier to forget about them than to reevaluate them.

All right, Manuel, I understand goals are important but where do I start? Funny you should ask. Understand that people approach goals in many different ways. I will show you how I approach mine and you can use my system or adapt it to a way that works for you. I hope you enjoy my way. If not, at least you'll have a good starting point for your way. Now in the following section, write down all your dreams. Remember, when you dream you can do anything and everything. Time and money are not considerations. Write down all your dreams. For example, on my list, I want an exotic car collection. I also want to travel the whole world. I want to own and manage a multimillion dollar company. Those are just a few. Now take the time and write your own.

THE GREATEST THING IN THIS WORLD IS NOT
SO MUCH WHERE WE ARE, BUT IN WHAT
DIRECTION WE ARE MOVING.
                    —OLIVER WENDELL HOLMES

DREAMS
1. Exotic car collection
2. Travel the world
3. Own a multimillion dollar company
4.
5.
6.
7.
8.
9.
10.
11.
12.
13.
14.
15.
16.

If you have more than 16 dreams continue on the back half of the paper.

Great. You are done with your dream sheet. Later, go back and spend as much time as you need and list all your dreams.

I have over 100 on my list. (It will take some time but you're worth it.)

Now let's write out some goals. Here's how to do it.

GOAL
Who?_____
What?_____
When?_____
Where?_____
Why?_____
How?_____

MY PAST DOES NOT HAVE TO
EQUAL MY FUTURE.

It is essential that you do this for every one of the goals you want to create action for. You will notice that some of your dreams will also be goals. The difference is a goal is something you work on. Every day a goal is followed by action.

Now, let's set a goal by following these steps. First, answer this question, "**whose**" goal is it? This must be *your* goal. No one else's. You will not commit or dedicate yourself if it is not your goal. So under "**Who**"?, put your name.

Now, you must specifically put "**what**" you want. Be specific. "A big house" or "a sports car" won't do. A fireball red 1997, 355 Ferrari convertible with CD player, rims, high performance tires, tint, cruise, air, top of the line alarm (name the alarm), black interior, 5 speed, and twin turbo carburetor. You get the point. Be specific. Yes, this is necessary. If you can't do this, there is no way that you can be excited about a goal.

Next, write down "**when**" you want it. Remember, it's great to think big and have powerful goals, but don't make unrealistic dates. If you want that Ferrari and you are riding the bus, then next month would probably be an unrealistic date. If you're planning to do it in three years, then pick a date three years from now. Goals are not unrealistic but dates can be, so be careful and set realistic dates. You get discouraged and disappointed because we don't give ourselves ample time to attain our goals. That's also a reason you should have short-term goals. You need to celebrate those short-term goals to keep you focused on those long-term goals.

"**Where**" is the next step. Where is the place you list the people, resources, and places you must go, speak to or visit to realize your vision. For example, if your goal is that Ferrari mentioned above then the first place you should go is the dealer, where you will talk to the salesman about the cost and get all the specifics you need. Next, you may visit with people who own one and ask them how they went about obtaining theirs.

"**Why**" is the next step, and this one is important because it will remind you every day when you read your goals why you are willing to commit to them. Is it power, prestige, to make you

DON'T JUST STAND THERE, MAKE
SOMETHING HAPPEN.
—LEE IACOCCA

"happy," to give you security? Why?

Last, but not least: "**How**". This is where you will develop a plan of action. This is where you will list the steps that you will take to make sure your goal is realized and not a dream waiting to happen.

Now go back to the "Who" line after you finish developing the steps and sign next to your name. I repeat; this is necessary. I really mean it. Commit yourself and make it work for you. Only 3 percent of Americans have goals and those 3 percent are the ones we envy. I'm just kidding. I don't envy them, but I do learn from them, and so should you. Here is how a goal should look.

GOAL

WHO?   MANUEL DIOTTE

WHAT?   1997 RED FERRARI CONVERTIBLE,
          355 CD PLAYER, ALPINE ALARM, SMOKED TINTED
          WINDOWS, BEIGE INTERIOR, CRUISE CONTROL,
          AIR, 5 SPEED, TILT, PHONE AND AIR BAGS.

WHEN?   MY BIRTHDAY, MAY 20, 2003

WHERE?   MOTOR IMPORTS, BANK, & MR. GARRETT

WHY?   IT IS THE MOST BEAUTIFUL CAR I'VE SEEN AND I
          WILL LOOK GREAT IN IT. I AM WORTH IT AND I
          DESERVE IT.

HOW: 75 SPEAKING ENGAGEMENTS A YEAR AT MY FULL
          FEE. INCREASE SAVINGS BY 17%

Do that with all your goals. You must keep these in places or rooms you visit often. Read them at least three times a day. You should be excited about them. Remember, these goals are non-negotiable. Be willing to do whatever it takes; providing, it's ethical, legal and moral, of course. Again, this will take up quite a bit of time. Take some time off and do this. It will make a difference and put you at the top. It's also important that you realize that there are, literally all kinds of goals; health, cultural, family, spiritual, economical, career, self-improvement, income, and more. I suggest you keep things simple. List them either under personal

THERE ARE THREE WAYS OF DOING THINGS.
1. DO IT YOURSELF.
2. HIRE SOMEONE TO DO IT.
3. TELL YOUR KIDS NOT TO DO IT.

such as family, or business, such as income. Keep it simple.

Next we will list our **values**. Let me explain what I mean. Values are choices we make. For instance, if someone drops a twenty-dollar bill in front of you, you will have to make a choice—to tell him or to pocket it. Your value system will determine what you will do. If you value honesty, then you will pick it up and return it. If you don't, then reaching a goal will not have the same satisfaction for you as it will for the honest person.

I strongly believe that if I have to break or compromise a value to reach a goal, then it's a goal not worth reaching. If I have to hurt somebody to buy my car then my car is not worth it. So, go ahead and write out some values.

VALUES
1. Honesty
2. Family
3. Never hurting anyone
4. Sharing
5. Respect
6. Friends
7. Love
8. _____
9. _____

*Values are non-negotiable, they're not up for discussion or debate.

Before we continue, allow me to share with you a little story about knowing what we know, without realizing that we know it. Confused? Let me explain.

In 1987, when I turned 18, I got a piece of paper and started writing down all my goals. As you already know one of my goals is that red Ferrari, with all the bells and whistles. So I went to the Ferrari dealer and asked to see the Testarossa. He showed it to me, inside and out. I sat in it and imagined myself driving it. The salesman thought I was crazy, but I didn't mind. After all, I drove up in a car that got me from point A to point B 80% of the time. I

IN YOUR SEARCH FOR RICHES,
DON'T LOSE THE THINGS THAT MONEY
CAN'T BUY.

then asked the salesman if he would take a picture of the Ferrari with me in it. By this time he thought I had lost it so, I explained this is my goal. I still carry that picture every day.

One day I was at a seminar and the speaker was talking about goals and how you should visualize your goal with pictures of it, whenever a picture was possible. By accident, I yelled out "I did that". The room then got church quiet and I apologized to the speaker and the room. I said, "I'm sorry, I was just excited." The speaker then said, "You have nothing to apologize for, because you're now one step above everyone in this room." You see, I was on the right track all the time without realizing it. You're on the right track, too. Obviously, you have read this far, and that tells me something great about you. So, lastly take a picture and look at it daily, several times if you have to get that extra charge. Feel that extra lift and go get 'em! I've also learned never to brag about my goals and what I'm going to do. It turns people off. I used to brag, only to look foolish later because it took more time than I thought. Besides, you don't need the negative attitudes people will display if you intimidate them. Share your goals with your encouragement club, the people who will support you. As for the others, results have a way of informing the world. Never wait for something to fall in your lap. Make it happen! I know you can! Do it now! Don't wait!

There are no short cuts or easy ways to achieve your goals. Achievement will require hard work, dedication, commitment and persistence. Don't be tempted to do the wrong things and take the easy way out. It takes a lot more energy to explain why you cheated than to explain the right way of doing it. Have the self-discipline to do the right thing. Your reward will be a great feeling of satisfaction, knowing you can and that you did.

Don't sell yourself out because it's a much better feeling to achieve with class and dignity than to compromise your self-respect.

THINK GOD!

Last, but not least, don't forget the people less fortunate. CARE FOR OTHERS MORE THAN PEOPLE THINK IS WISE.... Make specific goals to help others. As Zig Ziglar would say, *"You can get everything in life you want if you will help enough other people get what they want."*

Finally, always *DARE TO DREAM*. After you accomplish one goal, go after another goal.

Try new things! Take chances on your thoughts and remember, if you fail the first time, you're running about average. Or as humorist Newt Heilscher once said, "If at first you don't succeed, destroy all evidence that you tried." Remember, if you follow these basic steps you're sure to "hit" every time.

GOAL
1. Who? Whose goal is it?
2. What? What specifically?
3. When? When do I want it?
4. Where? Where will I go to get the resources necessary to make it happen?
5. Why? Why am I willing to commit?
6. How? How will I do it? Remember, you were born to win. You have what it takes, now take it and run!!!!

A SIGN ON A CHURCH BULLETIN—
IF YOU HAVE TROUBLES, COME IN AND
TELL US ABOUT THEM. IF YOU HAVE NONE,
COME IN AND TELL US HOW YOU DID IT.

Chapter Eleven

A Standing Ovation

After prescribing medicine for the patient the doctor said, "Let me know how it works. I'm having the same symptoms myself."

As I reflect on the big "C," I always come to the same conclusion, that being blessed with cancer has been one of the most rewarding experiences in my life. As you can tell, this book isn't just about cancer. It's about a way of life that works for me. It's a "winning" formula you might say. I share it with you because I really want the best for you. I really want you to enjoy life as I do, come what may. If I could write you a prescription for coping with your challenges it would all boil down to this: Celebrate each day, not with champagne, beer, wine, caviar or escargot but with smiles, kisses, hugs, high-fives, laughter, joy, excitement, and never forget the power of prayer.

It's a shame that so many people cripple their potential with self-pity. There's no time for pity parties. Be thankful everyday. Take one day at a time. Stop and smell the roses. Look at the sun, the moon, a rainbow, the stars and the beauty around you.

You have an awesome amount of power within you, a force of energy that, once focused in the right direction, will be unstoppable. Be willing to go out there and take a chance. After all you deserve it!!!

It was Mark Twain who said, "Thousands of geniuses live and die undiscovered either by themselves or by others." Don't let that happen to you.

I don't ask "why" anymore, because I have found my answer. Why not me? I can handle it. However, the real answer is really a question. What am I going to do about it? The choice is ours.

I know that the only handicap we have is right between our ears. The only blindness we have is the inability to see the great-

I CAN DO ALL THINGS THROUGH CHRIST
WHICH WILL STRENGTHEN ME.
—HOLY BIBLE- PHILLIPPIANS
CHAPTER 4:13

ness in ourselves. I also realize more than ever the importance of my faith. We don't have to go around trying to justify and ratify everything. I do believe that I was blessed with cancer and that it did happen for a reason. I know that my experience counted for something. I believe that it did with all my heart. I believe that there is a plan for me.

I don't believe I was punished for something I did at the age of six anymore than I believe that if I do something bad that I'll have bad luck tomorrow or in the future because God is going to come down on me. I don't think God has time to get even. I do believe that we tend to blame the wrong person (God) every time something bad happens. My God is a father of love, not hate. He doesn't sit in heaven watching every one of us waiting for us to do something wrong and BAM! Step on us.

It's not funny that He always gets the blame, as if He wants children to be born with birth defects, or that He's responsible for an innocent teen to die on his prom night because of some drunk driver. No, God doesn't cause that stuff to happen, man does.

It does seem that everyone knows what He wants all the time. People are always making naive statements about what He does and doesn't want.

Once again we're pointing the finger at the wrong man. If you're wondering if I ever asked "God why me?" I have and I was angry when I said it, only to feel guilty for questioning my Master.

It's amazing that everyone except the person suffering seems to know what God wants. But even during my questions, not once did I lose my faith. I always believed He loved me and never in my worst imagination did I feel He was punishing me as a child or adult.

Lastly, I give you a standing ovation (I really am standing). I thank you for your time and energy and I know this is the beginning of a whole new way of thinking, and as I reflect on my memories of cancer, I leave you with some more of my beliefs that have helped me succeed. I hope they help you.

SOMETIMES WINNING ISN'T BEING FIRST,
SOMETIMES WINNING IS JUST FINISHING.
—MANUEL

I believe good is better than evil.

I believe we must be a friend to have a friend. We must give love to receive love, in that order.

I believe losers blame circumstances, while winners rise above them.

I believe we need to remind the people we love that we love them.

I believe we need to take time to care about others less fortunate.

I believe we should all share.

I believe that with passion, sweat, tears, faith and determination you can live your dreams.

And I believe......

Happiness Is a Pair of Shorts!

I challenge you to put your shorts on, develop that positive attitude, smile and laugh about life like never before. Get past the fear that's holding you. Always keep your chin up and never, ever lose your faith. You have to go through the fire to come out steel. Go be the winner you were born to be. It starts when you believe!!!!!!!!!!

**MEET THE ONE WHO WENT TO BAT AGAINST
THE TOUGHEST ODDS.**

THROUGH THE YEARS,
MANUEL HAS BECOME A REAL INSPIRATION TO
US ALL. HELPING THOUSANDS. EACH OF HIS
PRESENTATIONS ARE ENRICHED WITH HUMOR,
ENTHUSIASM, AND LOTS OF FUN.

LET MANUEL
SHOW YOU HOW TO BELIEVE IN YOURSELF,
GET PAST THE FEAR THAT HOLDS YOU, AND HELP
YOU DISCOVER AND DEVELOP THE GIFTS AND BLESSINGS
WITHIN YOU, SO YOU CAN TURN YOUR
DREAMS INTO REALITY!!!!

AS A SPEAKER AND SEMINAR LEADER,
MANUEL IS TRULY A GRAND SLAM
HITTER. SO CALL AND MAKE YOUR NEXT
MEETING SPECTACULAR.

210.479.4128

For additional products go to
www.manueldiotte.com

Journal

express yourself . . .